DATE DUE

Indian Trail Jr. High LRC
Addison, IL

Aliens
Andrew Coddington

Cavendish Square
New York

CREATURES OF FANTASY
Aliens

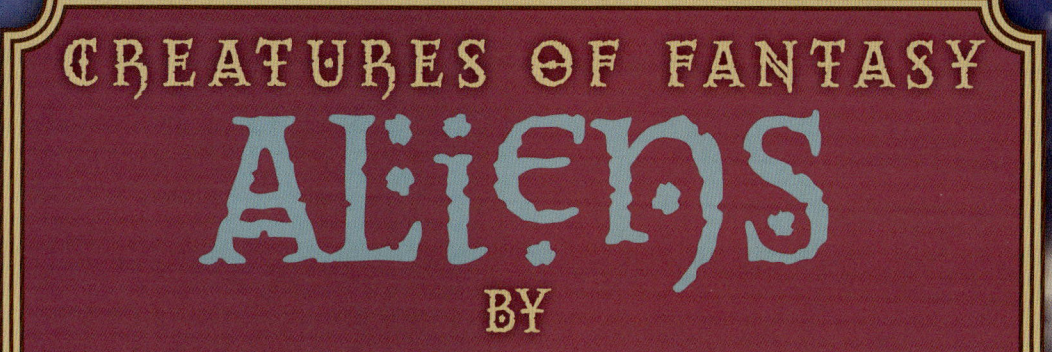

BY

ANDREW CODDINGTON

CAVENDISH SQUARE PUBLISHING · NEW YORK

Published in 2017 by Cavendish Square Publishing, LLC
243 5th Avenue, Suite 136, New York, NY 10016

Copyright © 2017 by Cavendish Square Publishing, LLC

First Edition

No part of this publication may be reproduced, stored in a retrieval system, or transmitted in any form or by any means—electronic, mechanical, photocopying, recording, or otherwise—without the prior permission of the copyright owner. Request for permission should be addressed to Permissions, Cavendish Square Publishing, 243 5th Avenue, Suite 136, New York, NY 10016. Tel (877) 980-4450; fax (877) 980-4454.

Website: cavendishsq.com

This publication represents the opinions and views of the author based on his or her personal experience, knowledge, and research. The information in this book serves as a general guide only. The author and publisher have used their best efforts in preparing this book and disclaim liability rising directly or indirectly from the use and application of this book.

CPSIA Compliance Information: Batch #CS16CSQ

All websites were available and accurate when this book was sent to press.

Cataloging-in-Publication Data

Names: Coddington, Andrew.
Title: Aliens / Andrew Coddington.
Description: New York : Cavendish Square, 2016. | Series: Creatures of fantasy | Includes index.
Identifiers: ISBN 9781502618627 (library bound) | ISBN 9781502618634 (ebook)
Subjects: LCSH: Life on other planets--Juvenile literature. | Unidentified flying objects--Juvenile literature.
Classification: LCC QB54.C63 2016 | DDC 576.8'39--dc23

Editorial Director: David McNamara
Editor: Kristen Susienka
Copy Editor: Rebecca Rohan
Art Director: Jeffrey Talbot
Designer: Joseph Macri
Senior Production Manager: Jennifer Ryder-Talbot
Photo Research: J8 Media

The photographs in this book are used by permission and through the courtesy of: Science Picture Company/Getty Images, cover; Mike Agliolo/Getty Images, 2-3; Science Photo Library/Superstock, 6; Scacciamosche/Getty Images, 8; John A. Davis, Shutterstock.com, 11; Roberto Gonzalez/Getty Images, 13; David Teter/Getty Images, 14; Craig Cozart/Getty Images, 16; DanitaDelimont/Getty Images, 19; Sharptoyou/Shutterstock.com, 21; Encyclopaedia Britannica/UIG22/Getty Images, 22; Barney Wayne/Keystone/Getty Images, 24; lassedesignen/Shutterstock.com, 27; USAF/Getty Images, 30; Digital Vision/Getty Images, 31; Ian Murray/Getty Images, 32; USAF/AFP/Getty Images, 35; USAF/AP Images, 36; Fortean/TopFoto/The Image Works, 41; Harry Warnecke/NY Daily News via Getty Images, 42; Hulton Archive/Getty Images, 46; (Inset) File: Martian face viking cropped.jpg - Wikimedia Commons/NASA-JPL, NASA-JPL digital version © Science Faction/Getty Images, 47; AF archive/Alamy, 48, 50; Universal/Archive Photos/Getty Images, 52; Fox/Liaison/Getty Images, 54; Gabe Ginsberg/Film Magic/Getty Images, 56; © Photos 12/Alamy, 58.

Printed in the United States of America

CONTENTS

INTRODUCTION 6

ONE
THE UNIVERSAL NEIGHBORHOOD 9

TWO
ALIENS THROUGH HISTORY 17

THREE
LIGHTS IN THE NIGHT SKY 25

FOUR
THE ROSWELL AND RENDLESHAM INCIDENTS 33

FIVE
THE SKIES ARE FALLING! 43

SIX
EXTRATERRESTRIALS IN FILM 49

SEVEN
ALIENS AMONG US 55

Glossary 60
To Learn More about Aliens 61
Bibliography 62
Index 63
About the Author 64

INTRODUCTION

Has Earth been visited by strange spacecraft piloted by alien beings?

Since the first humans walked Earth, myths and legends have engaged minds and inspired imaginations. Ancient civilizations used stories to explain phenomena in the world around them, such as the weather, the tides, and natural disasters. As different cultures evolved, so too did their stories. From their traditions and observations emerged creatures with powerful abilities, mythical intrigue, and their own origins. Sometimes, different cultures encouraged various manifestations of the same creature. At other times, these creatures and cultures morphed into entirely new beings with greater powers than their predecessors.

Today, societies still celebrate the folklore of their ancestors—on-screen in TV shows and movies such as *Doctor Who*, *Once Upon a Time*, and *Star Wars*, and in books such as the *Harry Potter* and *Twilight* series. Some even believe these creatures truly existed and continue to walk the earth as living creatures. Others resign these beings to myth.

In the Creatures of Fantasy series, we celebrate captivating stories of the past from all around the world. Each book focuses on creatures both familiar and unknown: the elusive alien, the grumpy troll, the devious demon, the graceful elf, the spellbinding wizard, and the harrowing mummy. Their various incarnations throughout history are brought to life. All have their own origins, their own legends, and their own influences on the imagination today. Each story adds a new perspective to the human experience and encourages people to revisit tales of the past in order to understand their presence in the modern age.

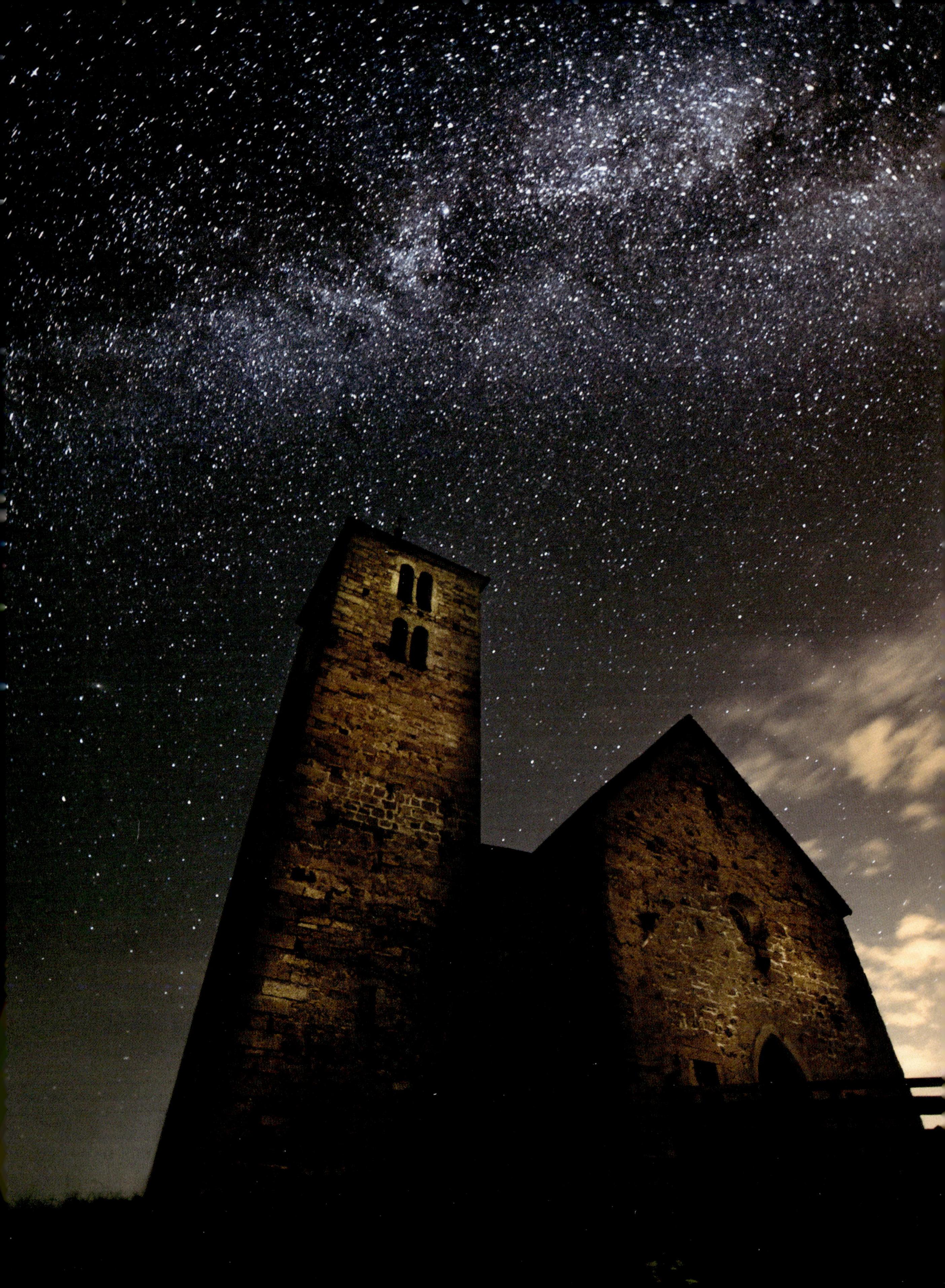

THE UNIVERSAL NEIGHBORHOOD

"A long time ago, in a galaxy far, far away . . . ."
STAR WARS

UMANS HAVE BEEN LOOKING UP AT THE stars for millennia as they try to understand Earth's place in the cosmos. For many thousands of years, people thought that what could be seen with the naked eye was all there was—flat land under a huge dome of sky with pinpricks of light. However, with the help of new technologies, our knowledge grew rapidly, and the known boundaries of the universe grew, too. Through the help of inventions like the telescope and space probes, humans came to see that the universe is much, much more than we could have ever imagined. Earth is a tiny planet in a small **solar system** orbiting around an average sun. Our sun is just one

Opposite: With a universe as large as ours, it's natural for Earthlings to wonder if we are alone.

of *billions* of other stars in our **galaxy**, though, and our typical galaxy is just one of hundreds of billions of other galaxies, each with their own numbers of stars and solar systems—and that's just in the parts of the universe that we can currently observe. Earth is like a single molecule of water in the Atlantic Ocean. Even with our advanced modern technology, scientists have not even begun to scratch the surface of what is out there. Given this extraordinary expanse of space we find ourselves in, we're left to wonder: are we alone?

A Great, Big Universe

The universe is so big that it is practically impossible for humans to fully grasp its size. Scientists estimate that the universe is 28 billion **light-years** in diameter. Think about switching on a light in a room. It seems to fill the room instantly, but light actually travels at a certain speed—it just happens to be so fast that it can fill a whole room without your eye even noticing. A light-year measures how far light travels in a whole year. Because light is so fast, it can cross a huge expanse of space within that time. Even using this extreme measurement, it still would take 28 billion years for light to reach from one end of the universe to the other.

Given how large the universe is, it seems likely that it must host some sort of **extraterrestrial**, or alien, life in addition to our own here on Earth. In fact, many prominent scientists, including the renowned astrophysicist Stephen Hawking, believe that it makes more sense for life to exist on another planet somewhere in the universe than for it to only exist on Earth.

Reaching Out Through Time and Space

Many scientists and alien enthusiasts dream of the day when we can make contact with alien life forms. Several man-made space probes have been launched from Earth to explore beyond our solar system, and each day, scientists listen carefully for radio waves coming from the deepest parts of space. However, the idea of communicating with extraterrestrial life has many problems. On the one hand, there is the issue of time and space. The nearest galaxy that is like our home galaxy, the Milky Way, is the Andromeda galaxy. However, Andromeda is 2.2 million light-years away, meaning that it takes light—the fastest thing in the universe—from Andromeda 2.2 million years to reach Earth. Whenever scientists observe Andromeda, they're actually looking back in time, seeing Andromeda as it was 2.2 million years ago.

Observations in space are really observations into the history of space. That fact means that if some sort of alien civilization is eventually discovered in the Andromeda galaxy, we are only seeing

The universe is an incredibly huge place. Earth's home galaxy, the Milky Way, pictured in part here, is just one of hundreds of billions of galaxies.

it as it was *millions and millions* of years ago. Making contact with that civilization might mean sending radio waves out into space, but because radio waves travel through space at about the speed of light, it would take millions of years *more* for those waves to reach this alien civilization. And then, if these aliens wanted to send a transmission back, it would take even more time. Discovering this civilization, making contact, and receiving communication back could potentially take *billions* of years. That's a long time to wait for a message.

Of course, this assumes that the extraterrestrial life is intelligent, meaning that it is capable of thoughts and possibly communication. If alien life on a planet far, far away takes the form of simple, one-celled **organisms**—or beings that are more complex but that lack basic communication technology like radios—there may never be contact with alien life.

Traveling through the space between our solar system and another is also basically impossible. Light is the fastest known substance in the universe. It is made up of photons, which makes light unlike the substance of matter and allows it to travel at extraordinary speeds. However, it is a known scientific fact that the more **mass** an object has, the greater the energy needed to move it. Imagine throwing a ball at 30 miles per hour (48 kilometers per hour) versus trying to get a car moving at that same speed. It would take much more effort to move the car, which has more mass, than the ball. To get something as large as a spacecraft into **deep space** would require an incredible amount of energy.

Take the space shuttle, one of the most recent vehicles scientists have designed to carry human beings into space, as an example. A space shuttle weighs 165,000 pounds (74,842 kilograms) by itself—about forty-two times heavier than the average car. However, a space shuttle also needs rockets and fuel to propel it through Earth's atmosphere, canisters of oxygen, and other supplies for astronauts guiding the vessel. Once those have been added, the whole space shuttle, including its launch vehicle, weighs 4.4 million pounds (1.9 million kg)! The space shuttle was only designed for short missions just outside Earth's atmosphere. Getting a space shuttle to an alien civilization in another solar system or galaxy would require practically impossible amounts of fuel, oxygen, and supplies.

However, just because humans currently lack the ability to travel through space at great speeds doesn't mean that no other entity in the universe is capable of this monumental feat. Perhaps somewhere in the farthest corners of what we know about our universe there exists a civilization so advanced that they can travel unimaginable distances across space with ease. Who are these creatures? What might they look like? What might they want?

The space shuttle is the most advanced vehicle for human space exploration, but even the space shuttle cannot travel far beyond Earth's atmosphere.

Scientists use huge dish-shaped telescopes such as this one to listen for radio waves coming from the farthest reaches of space.

How Probable Is Alien Life?

In 1961, Frank Drake, an astronomer at the University of California at Santa Cruz, came up with an equation to calculate the likelihood of intelligent extraterrestrial life in our home galaxy, the Milky Way. Known as the Drake Equation, it looks like this:

$$N = R_* \times F_p \times N_e \times F_l \times F_i \times F_c \times L$$

N is the number of civilizations in the Milky Way whose electromagnetic signals, such as radio waves, are detectable.

R_* is the rate of formation of stars that can host life. Many stars are not suitable for life, either because they are too hot, too cool, too bright, too dim, and so on.

F_p stands for the fraction of suitable stars with planetary systems, such as our solar system.

F_l is the fraction of planets where life actually exists.

F_i is the fraction of those planets that host intelligent life. A planet may contain life, but only in the form of simple, single-cell organisms like bacteria. In order for us to communicate with extraterrestrial life, they must be intelligent.

F_c is the fraction of intelligent alien civilizations that have the technology to transmit signals of their existence. Intelligent aliens may exist, but if they don't have a means to communicate, we may never make contact.

L is the length of time these civilizations have been releasing signals into space.

This simple equation helps to stimulate reasoned discussion on the existence of intelligent extraterrestrial life. Although it deals with fractions of fractions of fractions, given the scale of our galaxy, it is still possible that there may be one intelligent alien civilization somewhere—our galactic neighbors.

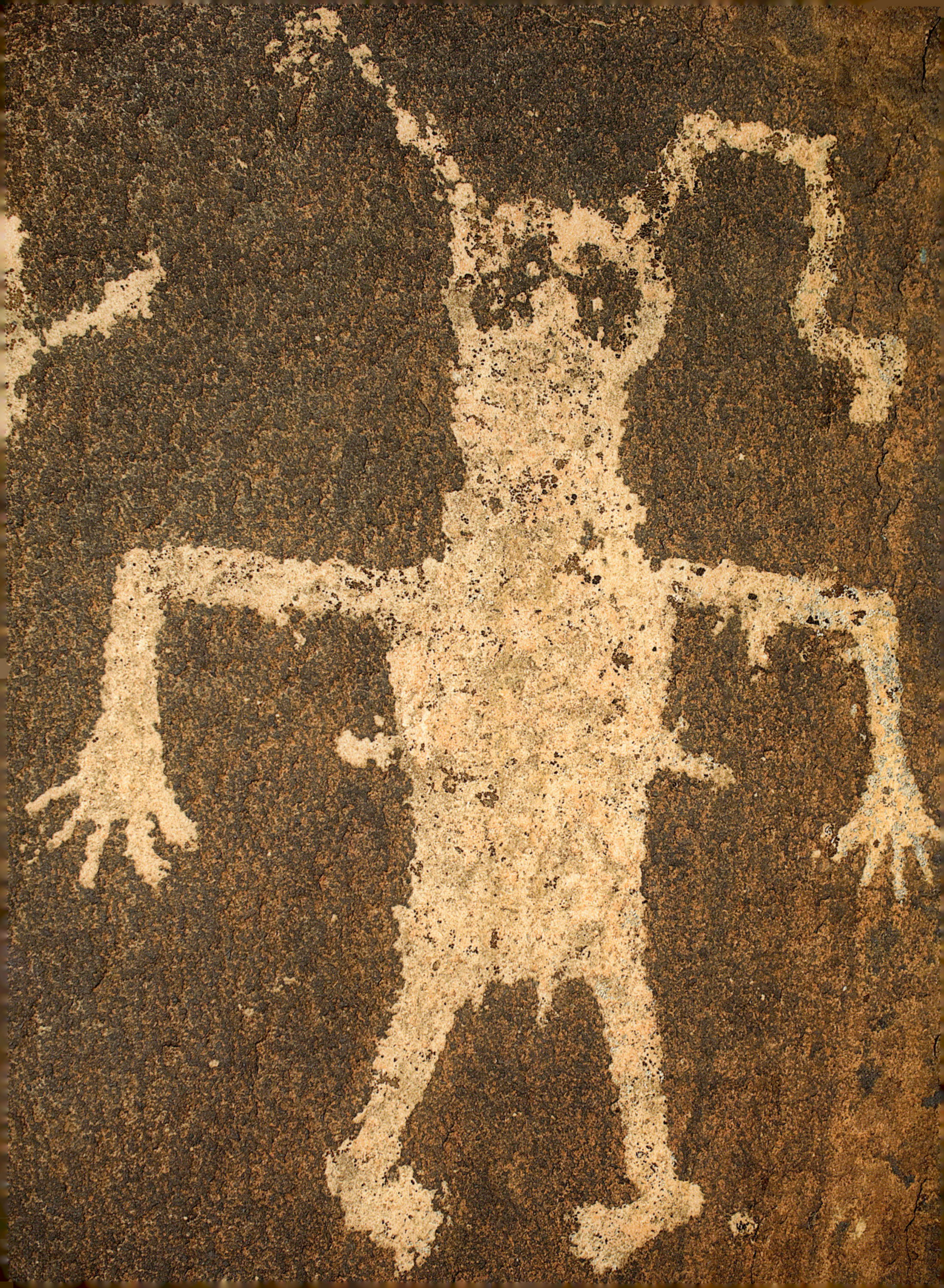

ALIENS THROUGH HISTORY

"Two possibilities exist: Either we are alone in the Universe, or we are not. Both are equally terrifying."

Arthur C. Clarke

ALIENS HAVE BEEN A PART OF THE HUMAN imagination from the very beginning of civilization. For as long as we have been gazing up at the stars, we have been wondering if there are other worlds inhabited by other beings like us—or nothing like us. Although many of our modern ideas of aliens come from movies, television, and books, ancient people had their own opinions on beings from space.

Origin Myths

Modern humans, called *Homo sapiens*, have only been around for about two hundred thousand years, and modern civilization for about six thousand years. When humans started to realize their place in a wider world, they wondered how exactly they came to be. Although

Opposite: Many ancient human cultures believed in the existence of otherworldly visitors. Some of these early peoples have left puzzling evidence, such as this rock art from Utah.

research into the fields of evolution and early anthropology has given us a pretty good idea of how we came to be, ancient humans did not have this understanding. As far as they could tell, there was no way of measuring how long humans had been on Earth, where they came from, or why they were here. Ancient cultures tried to answer these questions through stories called origin myths.

There are a variety of origin myths, but many ancient cultures told stories that were remarkably similar to one another. For example, many early humans believed that they were the product of superior beings called gods, who designed humans and put them on Earth to enjoy and work the lands. In the Judeo-Christian religious tradition, for example, one God created the world in seven days, then shaped the first human out of clay and breathed life into him.

Many of these origin stories about superior beings also mention that these creatures descended from the stars, much like aliens. The ancient Sumerian tradition has an especially interesting origin myth about celestial beings and their relationship with humans. The Sumerians were a people that built an impressive civilization in the area of modern-day Iraq and Iran around 4500 BCE. Their creation myth is recounted in clay tablets called the *Enuma Elish*. As the story goes, before there were humans, there were the gods, human-like beings who came down from the heavens to work the soil and mine for gold and other precious minerals. The gods realized that this was hard labor, however, so they created humans and taught them how to farm and mine. From their work, humans built civilization.

Ancient Astronauts

Where did the idea of sophisticated beings from the sky come from? Why do cultures around the world share this feature in their

Stonehenge (pictured here) is thought by some theorists to have been built by aliens.

origin stories? According to one theory, the answer is simple. This idea exists because it actually happened. Advanced beings from space really did come down to kick-start human civilization. This theory is known as the ancient astronaut theory.

According to the ancient astronaut theory, extraterrestrial life visited Earth thousands of years ago. When early humans first beheld these aliens, their incredible technology, and their sophisticated culture, they naturally saw them as gods. Over the centuries and across many cultures, these extraterrestrial beings guided Earthlings in the development of human culture. According to ancient astronaut theorists, everything from basic agriculture to huge building projects was the result of these visitors from outer space taking humans under their wing.

Ancient astronaut theorists often point to the great monuments of the ancient world, such as Stonehenge and the pyramids of Egypt and Mesoamerica, as proof of alien intervention. These monuments, they argue, are so incredibly complicated and required such exceptional feats of engineering that they could not have been built by ancient humans. In the case of Stonehenge, the largest of the rocks weigh an average of 25 tons (22.6 metric tons), which would be difficult for even modern machines to lift and place in a precise circle. Rather than lifting them with simple machines and brute strength, the ancient Britons had help from extraterrestrials.

It is important to keep in mind that the ancient astronaut theory, like many other subjects related to aliens, is considered a "fringe theory," meaning that it has not reached widespread acceptance among the scientific community. In fact, most people consider the ancient astronaut theory to be pseudoscience, or "fake science," because it does not follow the established method of scientific inquiry. Most science is based in facts, and from these facts scientists draw their conclusions. Ancient astronaut theorists work backwards, beginning with their conclusion—that aliens have visited Earth and directly influenced human culture—and then set out to find evidence that supports their conclusion. This is bad science because it leads people to only see evidence that supports their point, ignore evidence that is against it, and make connections that are not really there.

The Mysteries of the Nazca

The Nazca people, who inhabited Peru, South America, from the first century BCE to the early first century CE, are often used as evidence in support of the ancient astronaut theory. This ancient civilization left many puzzling aspects of their culture that few people today fully understand, which leads many to think they were influenced by an alien civilization.

One particularly fascinating aspect of Nazca culture are several huge geoglyphs, or formations made in the ground, called the Nazca Lines. These appear as either perfectly straight, miles-long lines or complex animal designs, such as an ant, a hummingbird, a dog, an eagle, and more, many of which are larger than a football field. The Nazca Lines are so large that they can only be seen as a whole from an aircraft.

One of the most famous of these formations depicts a human-shaped creature with one arm pointing to the ground, another pointing to the sky, and a round head with two large eyes. Many people call this design the "owlman" or the "fisherman," but ancient astronaut theorists call it the "astronaut." They argue that the astronaut's round head and large eyes may either represent a space helmet or the facial features of an alien species. The being's two arms pointing to the ground and the sky suggest that either something has come down from the skies to Earth or something from Earth was taken into the sky.

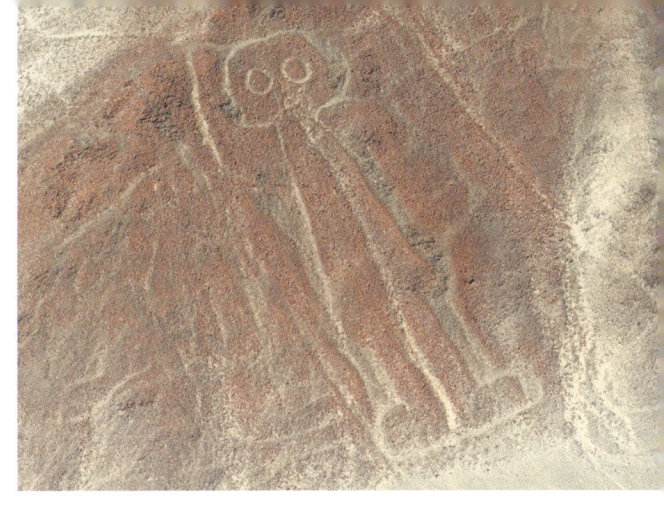

The Nazca "astronaut" is a popular piece of evidence for ancient astronaut theorists.

The Nazca people also participated in a unique body modification called trephination, or skull manipulation. Many traditional and modern cultures perform body modification, such as lip elongation practiced in many African and South American cultures and tattoos from everywhere to New Zealand to the United States. Nazca skull manipulation, however, involved a long, painful process whereby infants' heads were strapped to cushions and wooden boards. As the child aged, their skulls were forced into a different shape. This practice was the inspiration behind the movie *Indiana Jones and the Kingdom of the Crystal Skull*, which was directed by Stephen Spielberg and premiered in 2008. In this *Indiana Jones* film, the Nazca are alleged to have shaped their heads in order to mirror a race of alien visitors with elongated, pointed skulls.

Aliens in the Twentieth Century

Following World War II (1939–1945), the United States and several other countries started to devise plans to seriously explore space. The United States and the Soviet Union in particular sought to beat one another in claiming the honor of putting the first satellites in orbit, the first man in space, the first crew on the moon, and so on, a competition that became known as the Space Race. Enormous amounts of money

The Martian landscape is barren, but many think it once held life.

and attention were put into space exploration throughout the 1950s and 1960s. This had an effect on popular culture. As Americans watched human astronauts suit up to expand the reaches of scientific understanding, they daydreamed about what sorts of things they might find in space. Many of those dreams included aliens.

People imagined that if extraterrestrial life existed anywhere in our solar system, it would be on Mars. Mars is the second-closest planet in our solar system to Earth (Venus is closer, but it is too hot and its atmosphere is too toxic to support life), so many people think that it may have at one time (or even at that time) hosted simple organic life forms similar to those found on our own planet. In fact, scientists now possess data collected by the Mars Curiosity Rover, which touched down in August 2012 to study the surface of the Red Planet, that points to the existence of water on Mars. Water is one of the essential building blocks of life, as we understand it. It may even be possible that Mars once had an atmosphere much like Earth's, and therefore was able to support life, before a process like global warming made it inhospitable.

America's obsession with Martians (the term for alien life on Mars) coincided with the rise of Hollywood, so many filmmakers chose nightmarish alien invaders as the subjects for their movies. Movies like *Invaders from Mars*, which was directed by William Cameron Menzies and was released in 1953, and George Pal's *The War of the Worlds*, which was released the same year, fueled people's fear about hostile creatures lurking on the Red Planet. The aliens in these movies took on different shapes, from tall, green human-like beings to unusual octopi-like creatures that crawled around on tentacles. In both cases, however, the extraterrestrials wielded technology unlike anything humans had seen—heat ray guns, giant walking tripod machines, and bulletproof spacecraft.

Biblical Aliens?

The Tanakh—or the Old Testament, as it is called in Christian traditions—is one of the foundational texts of the Jewish religion. In addition to documenting the early history of the Hebrew people, it may also contain evidence that points to the existence of aliens. The first chapter of the Book of Ezekiel, one of the books of the Torah, contains a passage that has puzzled many religious scholars:

> [T]he heavens were opened, and I saw visions of God ... As I looked—behold—a stormy wind came out of the north, and a great cloud, with brightness around it, and fire flashing forth continually, and in the midst of the fire, as it were gleaming metal. And from the midst of it came the likeness of four living creatures. And this was their appearance: they had a human likeness.

Many ancient astronaut theorists speculate that this passage actually describes an extraterrestrial spacecraft that visited the ancient Hebrews. It is important to keep in mind, however, that the Bible describes many miraculous encounters, and the writers often used fantastic and figurative language to describe them. It is possible that this passage is merely trying to describe the emotional experience of God rather than an actual historical event. Perhaps at the end of the day, as with other parts of the Bible, it is a question best left to faith.

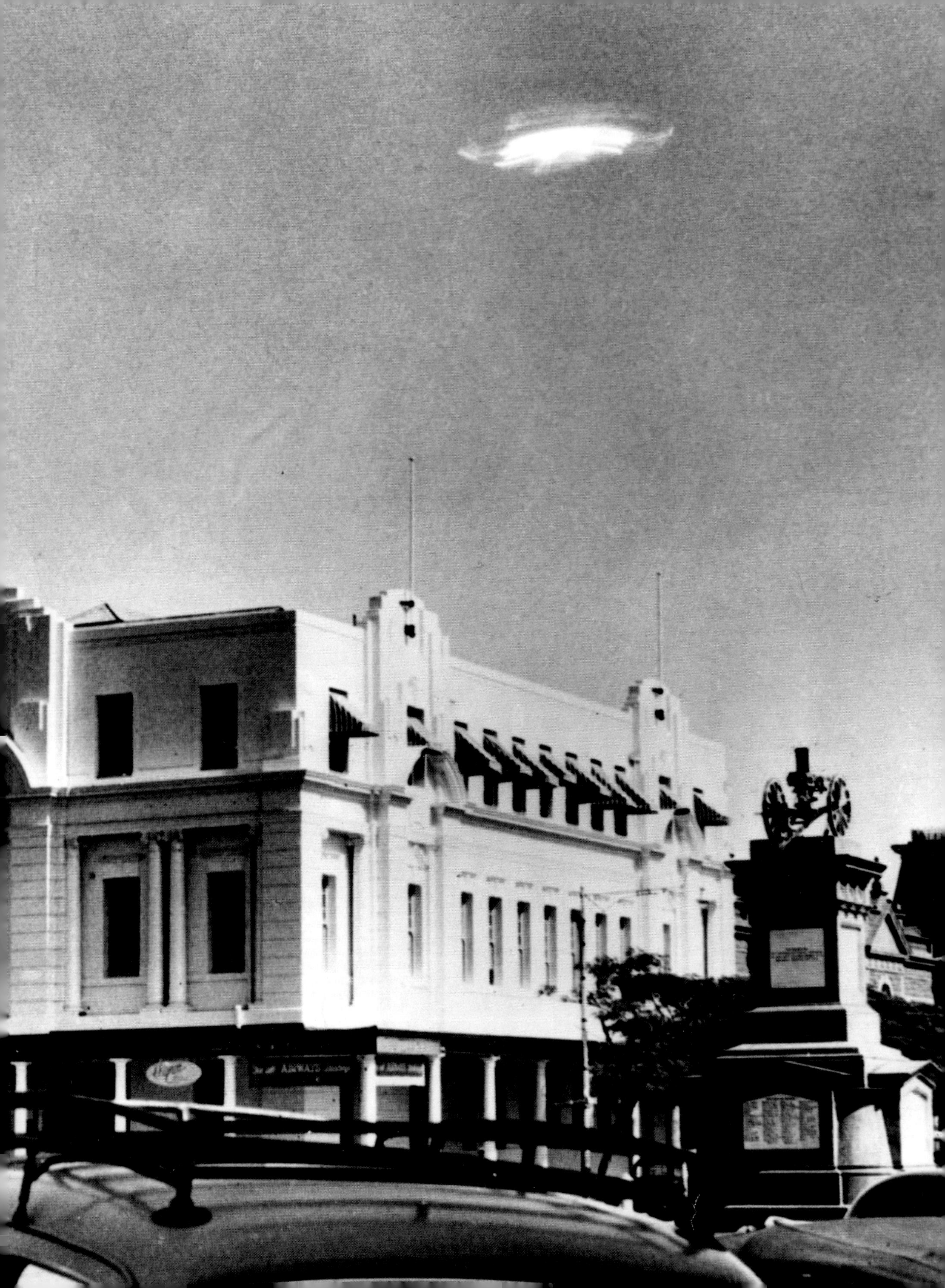

3

LIGHTS IN THE NIGHT SKY

"Perhaps we've never been visited by aliens because they have looked upon Earth and decided there's no sign of intelligent life."

Neil DeGrasse Tyson

Americans are split on alien belief. A poll conducted in 2013 by the Internet market research firm YouGov and sponsored by the *Huffington Post* found that 50 percent of Americans believe extraterrestrial life exists. Of the remainder, 17 percent do not believe, and 33 percent said they are not sure. While opinions on the reality behind aliens seem to be split among Americans, for some people, the existence of aliens is an all-too-real fact. These people not only claim to have encountered an alien but believe they were actually physically **abducted**, or taken, by them.

Opposite: A photo of an alleged spacecraft taken on December 29, 1953, in Bulawayo, South Africa

Alien Abductions

One of the first instances of an alien abduction to gain widespread attention was the case of Barney and Betty Hill. In September 1961, the Hills were traveling to their home in New Hampshire after a vacation in Canada. At some point during the night, the Hills noticed an unusually bright object shining in the sky, which they initially thought was a star. They pulled off to the side of the road to get a better look. Mr. Hill saw through a pair of binoculars that the object seem to be shaped like an oval, with multiple rows of different-colored lights and windows. The Hills were startled by the aircraft, so they got in their car and sped away. A little while later, they arrived home, but something didn't sit right with them. They checked the time and discovered it was two hours later than they thought.

Later that week, the Hills started to have nightmares about being kidnapped and operated on. Disturbed by the recurring dreams, they sought psychiatric help. Under the direction of their doctor, the Hills participated in hypnosis. While under the effects of their treatment, the Hills described how the object they had seen in the sky landed. Odd-looking men came out of it and dragged them, kicking and screaming, back into the craft. Then, they said, the creatures began to perform medical tests on them separately, before returning them to their car and sending them back on their way.

For the time being, the Hills had only shared their story with their family, close friends, and doctor. However, the story was leaked to a newspaper called the *Boston Traveler* four years later, setting off a media firestorm. The account of the Hills' abduction quickly reached every corner of the United States. Even serious ufologists (people who study aliens and **UFOs**) mentioned being deeply disturbed by the encounter.

There have been many people over the years who claim to have been abducted by aliens.

The Hills' abduction story is just one of dozens of similar accounts of humans being taken by aliens for research. Unfortunately, like the Hills' encounter, most such accounts lack crucial details, making them hazy at best. To those who believe in aliens, the reason abductees cannot recall their encounters may be because they were so frightened by the experience that their brain is blocking the memories. Others suggest that abductees have had their memories medically altered by their captors at some point during the encounter. However, to many **skeptics**, these explanations seem far-fetched. They argue that the reason abductees can't fully remember their experiences is because the abductions never actually happened. To skeptics, these stories were either made up, part of a dream, a misremembered memory, or an outright **hoax**.

Studying Abductees

Because the number of people who are willing to admit to being abducted is so small, it is difficult to study what about them made them candidates for alien abduction (or, for skeptics, what about them makes them *think* they've been abducted). However, there may be a general pattern across abduction stories. For one, most abductees are young people, usually under the age of forty. For many people over forty who have claimed to have had an alien encounter, they frequently say that they were "rejected" by the aliens, usually because of a medical condition. If these stories are to be believed, it seems extraterrestrials are interested in weeding out physically unfit human candidates. It may be that only young people with no medical issues are good subjects for alien studies.

Researchers have been unable to conclude whether or not alleged abductees have a higher likelihood of suffering from mental illness. One study concluded that people who report they have been abducted by aliens are more prone to having vivid nightmares and paranoia than the average person. This suggests that their accounts may have been influenced by an overactive imagination run wild in a sort of waking dream. However, another study said that the abductees surveyed did not show signs of any mental disorder. Both of these studies looked at only a small number of people, however, which means that their studies may be too small to adequately reflect the mental states of the whole range of abductees.

Unidentified Flying Objects

There are countless photos taken of alleged UFOs. These take on many forms, from the classic flying saucer to triangles and exotic shapes. All of these aircraft seem to be made of extremely smooth material, move silently through the sky, and are capable of dramatic aerial maneuvers, such as coming to full stops, hovering, accelerating extremely quickly, and rapidly changing direction while traveling at full speed. Each of these, UFO believers note, are difficult for even modern aircraft to perform, and some, such as coming to complete stops or quickly changing direction at top speed, are physically impossible. Even more troubling, UFOs seem to be able to vanish at a moment's notice, gone as quickly as they appeared.

Debunking UFOs

Technically, a UFO is simply an unidentified flying object in the sky. This means that anything someone sees and cannot explain is a UFO. However, that does not mean that every UFO is actually an alien spacecraft visiting Earth. What may seem to be an alien spacecraft may be one of a number of little-known airborne **phenomena**. For example, a UFO may be a **classified** experimental military aircraft on a test flight. These aircraft are often unusually shaped, so when people who are unaware of the test see them in the sky, they don't recognize them as a man-made plane. Furthermore, these aircraft often contain new, powerful technologies, so when people ask the military if they have been testing experimental aircraft, the military will often refuse to comment in order to protect the integrity and secrecy of the project. This silence fuels speculation that the military is actually hosting alien spacecraft.

Experimental aircraft played a part in building the myth behind Area 51, located in Nevada. From the mid-1950s on, Area 51 served as the base for testing new aircraft, such as the U-2 spy plane, as well as a training ground for new pilots. The U-2 was capable of flying at 60,000 feet (18,288 meters), a height at the time thought impossible for aircraft to achieve. When civilians spotted the U-2 high in the atmosphere, they feared it was an alien spaceship. Because the U-2 plane was classified, those at Area 51, as well as other military organizations investigating the claims,

Experimental military aircraft, such as the B-2 stealth bomber, are often mistaken for alien spaceships.

could not admit to the tests, so the rumor that Area 51 was attracting extraterrestrials grew.

Other explanations for alleged UFOs are atmospheric phenomena. It is sometimes possible for atmospheric conditions to combine in such a way that they create shapes that can be mistaken for UFOs. One such phenomenon is ball lightning. Ball lightning is a sphere of electrical charge that glows intensely, often for minutes at a time. Like other types of electricity, ball lightning is often attracted to metal objects, such as planes. Sometimes ball lightning will "chase" a metal plane, while other times it will fly about erratically—both common descriptions of alleged UFOs. While not much is understood about ball lightning or under what circumstances it forms, it is nevertheless a well-documented natural occurrence and not an example of alien visitors.

Another fascinating phenomenon behind many UFO sightings is lenticular clouds. These clouds form at very high altitudes, usually where moist air flows over a mountaintop. Under certain circumstances, these clouds can take on a round, lens-like shape—much like that of a UFO.

Statistically, ninety-nine of one hundred alleged UFOs can be easily explained away with one of these natural or man-made phenomena. However, there is still the 1 percent that remains unexplained. Once the hoaxes and misunderstandings have been eliminated, there remains a handful of genuinely concerning encounters that simply defy explanation.

Crop circles can take a variety of shapes.

Crop Circles

A popular piece of evidence that many believe points to the existence of extraterrestrials are **crop circles**. These interesting formations have been reported to mysteriously appear in farmers' fields for decades. Crop circles, as their name suggests, are generally circular in shape and are formed by flattening the stalks of the plant being grown in the field. Some are as simple as a single, perfect circle, while others take on the appearance of advanced mathematical formulae or even animals, such as an ant, a snake, and a jellyfish.

Sadly, many crop circles are confirmed hoaxes. A team of humans can replicate even the most detailed crop patterns by pressing down the stalks with a wooden board over the course of a night. In fact, the United Kingdom-based organization Circlemakers openly discusses the design and construction of a successful crop circle. They have also taken credit for most crop circles that appear in that country. However, there are a handful of crop circles whose creation remains a mystery, either because the manner of the stalks' flattening was not crushed, as would happen with a human and a board, or because the circles give off some unusual radioactive pulses.

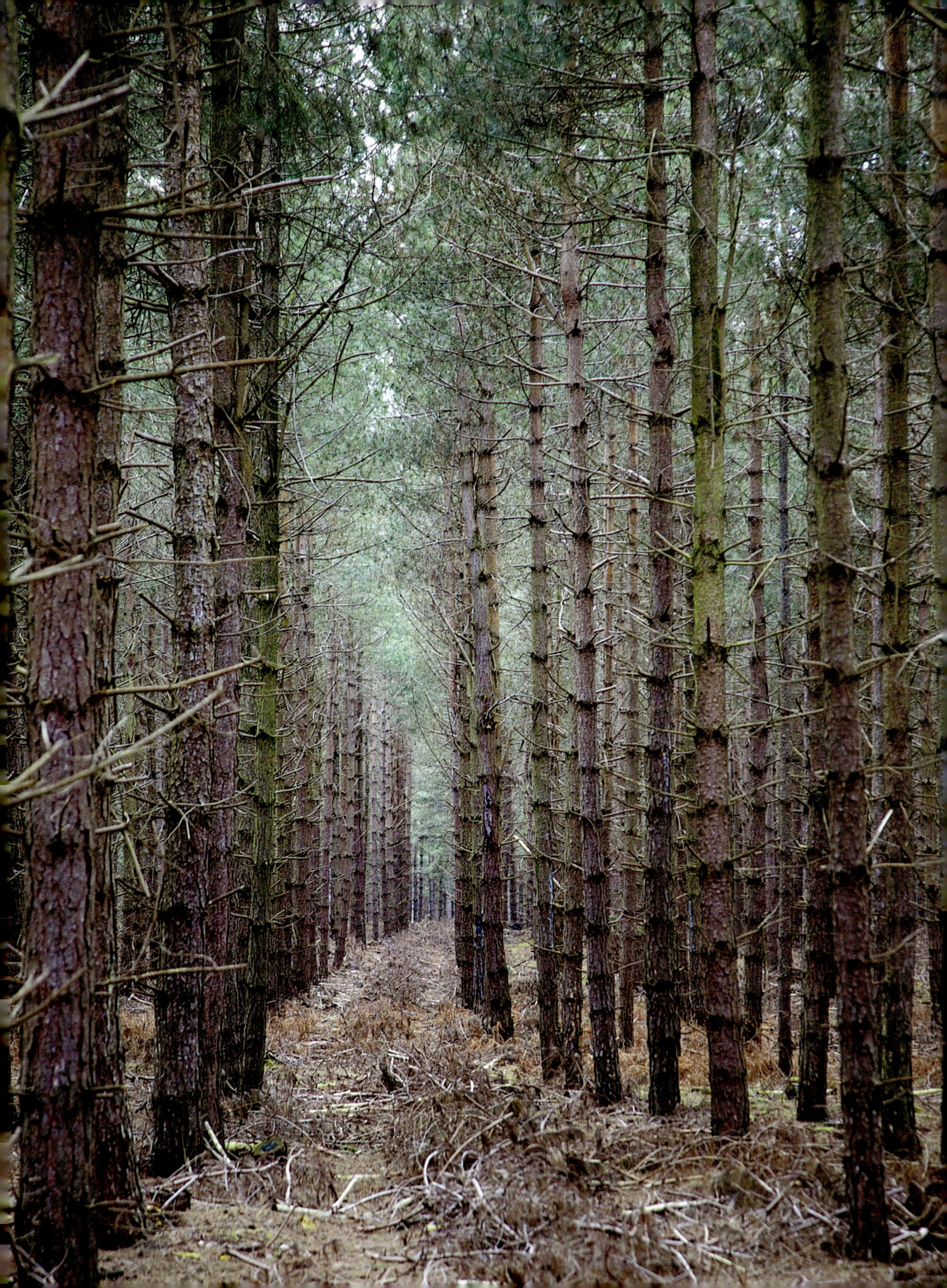

THE ROSWELL AND RENDLESHAM INCIDENTS

"ATTENTION ALBUQUERQUE: CEASE TRANSMISSION. REPEAT. CEASE TRANSMISSION. NATIONAL SECURITY ITEM. DO NOT TRANSMIT. STAND BY."

Unidentified government authority demanding radio stations stop broadcasting news regarding Roswell, New Mexico, on the night of July 8, 1947

THE MOST FAMOUS UFO STORY OF ALL takes place in the small town of Roswell, New Mexico. In the summer of 1947, witnesses living around Roswell noticed a shiny, disc-shaped object flying quickly across the sky. Evidence shows that the military had also been tracking an unidentified object flying across New Mexico for days. On July 4, Roswell resident William Woody reported seeing a bright object plunge to the ground.

The next morning, William Brazel, a foreman on a sheep ranch, along with his neighbor, Timothy Proctor, came across a pile of odd debris in the sheep's grazing land. There were pieces of rubber, splinters of wood, and strange metal resembling

Opposite: Rendlesham Forest in Suffolk, United Kingdom

aluminum foil. It seemed like some sort of airplane had crashed and exploded. Brazel handled the debris and noted that it was unusually lightweight yet strong.

The day after, Brazel reported his discovery to the sheriff, George Wilcox, who in turn forwarded the report to Major Jesse Marcel, an intelligence officer at the Roswell Army Air Field. On July 7, Marcel, along with Captain Sheridan Cavitt, followed Brazel to the site where he said he found the debris. Marcel and Cavitt analyzed the debris and concluded that it must have been from an exploding aircraft, but the materials used were unlike any they were familiar with. The metal that was thin and flexible like tinfoil was also, Marcel said, indestructible. Marcel later said, "I didn't know what we were picking up. I still don't know what it was … I've seen rockets … It definitely was not part of an aircraft or missile or rocket."

Hiding the Evidence

On July 8, the Roswell Army Air Field gave a press release to two radio stations stating that the military had recovered a flying disc. Within hours, the Associated Press released the story, saying, "The Army Air Forces here today announced a flying disk [sic] had been found." The media jumped on the story, and soon newspapers and private individuals around the world were calling the airfield with requests for more information. Unfortunately, little more was to be confirmed by the military.

The mysterious debris was taken to the airfield and stored in Brigadier General Roger Ramey's office. Ramey was the commanding officer at the airfield, and he was scheduled to meet with his commanding officer about what was now rumored to be an alien spacecraft. However, some sources report that the debris was moved without Ramey's knowledge, and a wrecked weather balloon was put in its place. The airfield's original press release was later rescinded, or withdrawn, and radio stations broadcasting the original story were commanded by an unidentified government agent to cease their reports. The next day, a new press release was given to the media stating that the wreckage was actually from a crashed weather balloon, which was mistaken for a flying disc.

Major Jesse Marcel from the Roswell Army Air Field poses with the debris of an alleged UFO in 1947.

Proof of Alien Life?

The incident at Roswell may be the most famous account of an alien encounter, but it is also one of the most **debunked**. While there is clear evidence of a **cover-up** and **conspiracy**, the conclusion that what the government was trying to conceal from the public was the crash-landing of an alien spacecraft is wrong.

Many **conspiracy theorists** point to Roswell as evidence that the United States government not only knows about the existence of extraterrestrial life on Earth but also actively works to cover it up. They may have a point. On the one hand, there definitely seems to have been an effort by the military to keep information about the debris from reaching the public. On July 8, 1947, radio broadcasts reporting the story were ordered to cease transmitting. Mysteriously, the authority who issued the order has not been identified. Additionally, the official explanation that the debris came from a downed weather balloon seems to have been a lie.

Many conspiracy theorists argue that authorities in Roswell used "body bags" to transport remains of alien life forms.

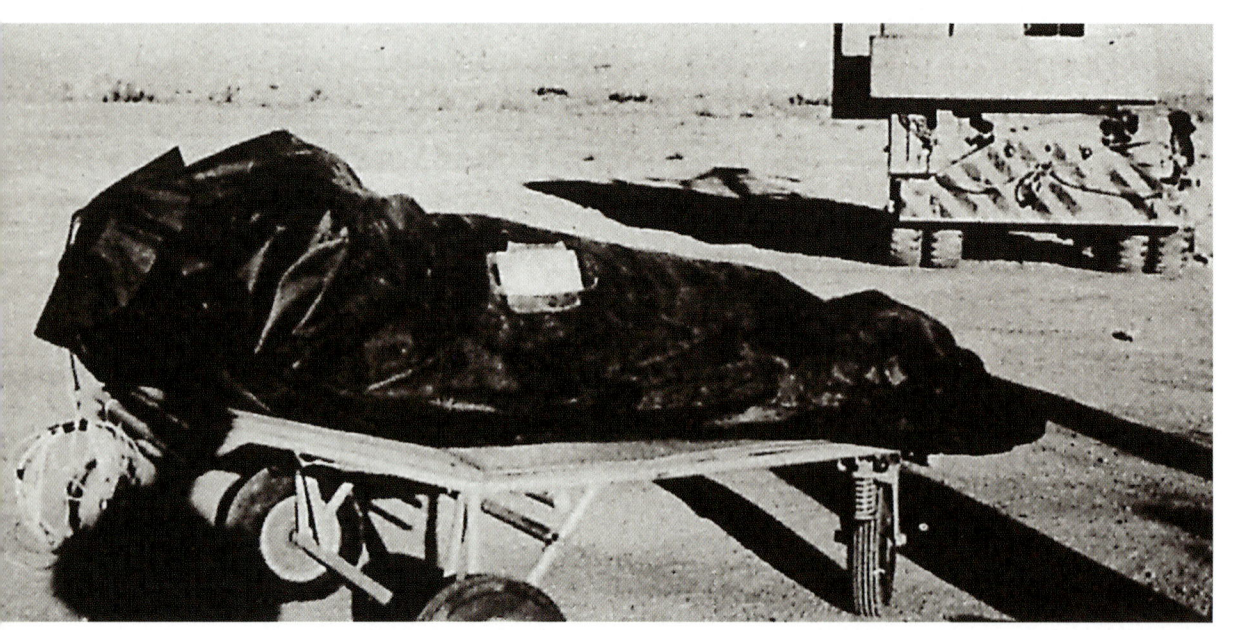

While the debris may not have been from a weather balloon, that doesn't automatically mean that it came from an alien spacecraft either. Disproving one possibility does not mean that the other explanation must be right. The government may have concealed the truth behind the debris, but there are other reasons that explain why the government would want to keep the event secret that do not include aliens.

In the case of Roswell, it was later revealed that the debris came from a downed balloon used in a top-secret military operation called Project Mogul. At the end of World War II, the relationship between the United States and the Soviet Union grew tense. Together with the invention of nuclear weapons, the United States and the Soviet Union became embroiled in the Cold War. The United States was fearful that the Soviet Union might develop their own nuclear weapons and potentially use them against the United States.

Project Mogul was one of the first secret operations the United States had organized to spy on the Soviets. It involved using microphones attached to high-altitude weather balloons, which would detect the sounds of explosions if the Soviets were testing nuclear weapons. The debris at Roswell came from one of these balloons, which lost altitude and crashed on Brazel's ranch. The US government had concealed the truth of the discovery to keep the Soviets from knowing that they were spying on them.

The Rendlesham Forest Incident

While the event at Roswell lacked much of the evidence to make it a valid case of UFO activity, another case has proven to be much stickier. It took place in Rendlesham Forest, located between two

United States Air Force bases on the east coast of England. Like Roswell, Rendlesham seems to be the target of a cover-up. What distinguishes this incident from the other, however, is the huge body of proof that something not of this world actually did touch down on Earth.

On the night of December 26, 1980, Airman First Class John Burroughs was keeping watch on the eastern gate of Woodbridge Air Force Base. Sometime shortly after midnight, Burroughs noticed strange lights in the sky. He reported seeing two lights, one blue and one red, one on top of the other, which flashed on and off as they descended into Rendlesham Forest. Burroughs initially thought the lights were coming from a downed aircraft, which was forced to land in the forest. However, when this theory was checked with the Air Marshall on duty at the time, it became clear that no military or civilian flights had been scheduled. The aircraft—if that's what it was—was unidentified. Burroughs ran his report up the chain of command at the bases, and after several quick radio and phone calls, Burroughs, along with Sergeant James Penniston and several others, was told to scout the forest for the source of the unexplained lights.

Because the first theory for the unexplained lights was a downed aircraft, the official reason for the scouting party was search and rescue. But the soldiers' behavior during the expedition seemed to indicate otherwise. First, they didn't call for an ambulance or even carry a medical kit to assist any injured pilots or passengers. Additionally, they carried their weapons into the forest. According to the agreement the United States had with the United Kingdom as a condition of operating the base, US soldiers could leave the base under certain circumstances, but it was only during imminent security threats that servicemen could carry their weapons with them. Because they did carry their weapons, it seems to indicate that they were fearful of something more serious. Lastly, the men were ordered to approach the crash site with "extreme caution."

The scouting party drove down the main road through the forest a short ways before turning down an access road. The path had become too rugged for their jeep to pass, so the men continued on foot. Their radios had started to malfunction, and they lost communication with the base. They chose one of their group to stay with the jeep so that they could "leapfrog" their reports, relaying short-range messages to the radio on the jeep, which could then report back to base. As they moved deeper into Rendlesham, the range on their radios got progressively worse. Each man in the party was asked to stay behind and relay messages in a long chain back to the jeep, leaving Burroughs and Penniston as the only two men who would continue to the site of the unidentified object.

As Burroughs and Penniston neared the crash site, a huge burst of light engulfed the forest. The two men dropped to the ground, fearing that there had been an explosion. Penniston slowly got back up and approached a clearing where he saw the source of the lights for the first time. There, among the thick trees of Rendlesham Forest, sat what could only be described as an alien spacecraft.

Penniston wrote down many details about what he saw in his pocket notepad. The craft was about 10 feet tall by 10 feet wide (3 m by 3 m), metallic, and triangle-shaped. It sat on a tripod, which had left deep markings on the ground. It was estimated by the depth of the gouges and the hardness of the ground that the craft must have weighed several tons. Around the middle of it was a ring of blue lights, and on top was a white light, which shone on him when he reached out to touch the craft. Penniston said the body of the craft was as smooth as glass and totally seamless. It was also marked with what he described as something like Egyptian hieroglyphics, which were rougher in texture.

Eventually, the craft began to lift off again. It maneuvered around the trees before taking off like a shot. Penniston described its flight in his book: "Speed—impossible." Just like that, the UFO was gone.

Neither Burroughs nor Penniston thought they had been in the forest for long, but by the time they returned to the base, their superiors were nervous, complaining that the two airmen had been gone too long without contact. When Burroughs and Penniston checked their watches, they discovered that both were running forty-five minutes slower than the time on the base clocks. Neither could account for the lost time, but both agreed that they did not feel as though they had been gone so long. Like the Hills before them, the American airmen had experienced unexplainable time loss.

Cover-Up

As with Roswell, someone seems to have tampered with the evidence regarding the event. Both Penniston and Burroughs had given field reports immediately after their experience. However, before they could be examined by the airfield's commanding officer, they had gone missing—someone had taken them.

The Rendlesham Forest incident, as it has become known, remains one of the most troubling encounters in the search for proof of aliens. The events that took place have been independently verified by a variety of well-regarded individuals, including two US airmen, who to this day are convinced that they made physical contact with an alien spacecraft. Either all of those people are lying or are mistaken about what they experienced, or aliens have landed on Earth.

DEPARTMENT OF THE AIR FORCE
HEADQUARTERS 81ST COMBAT SUPPORT GROUP (USAFE)
APO NEW YORK 09755

REPLY TO
ATTN OF: CD   13 Jan 81

SUBJECT: Unexplained Lights

TO: RAF/CC

1. Early in the morning of 27 Dec 80 (approximately 0300L), two USAF security police patrolmen saw unusual lights outside the back gate at RAF Woodbridge. Thinking an aircraft might have crashed or been forced down, they called for permission to go outside the gate to investigate. The on-duty flight chief responded and allowed three patrolmen to proceed on foot. The individuals reported seeing a strange glowing object in the forest. The object was described as being metalic in appearance and triangular in shape, approximately two to three meters across the base and approximately two meters high. It illuminated the entire forest with a white light. The object itself had a pulsing red light on top and a bank(s) of blue lights underneath. The object was hovering or on legs. As the patrolmen approached the object, it maneuvered through the trees and disappeared. At this time the animals on a nearby farm went into a frenzy. The object was briefly sighted approximately an hour later near the back gate.

2. The next day, three depressions 1 1/2" deep and 7" in diameter were found where the object had been sighted on the ground. The following night (29 Dec 80) the area was checked for radiation. Beta/gamma readings of 0.1 milliroentgens were recorded with peak readings in the three depressions and near the center of the triangle formed by the depressions. A nearby tree had moderate (.05-.07) readings on the side of the tree toward the depressions.

3. Later in the night a red sun-like light was seen through the trees. It moved about and pulsed. At one point it appeared to throw off glowing particles and then broke into five separate white objects and then disappeared. Immediately thereafter, three star-like objects were noticed in the sky, two objects to the north and one to the south, all of which were about 10° off the horizon. The objects moved rapidly in sharp angular movements and displayed red, green and blue lights. The objects to the north appeared to be elliptical through an 8-12 power lens. They then turned to full circles. The objects to the north remained in the sky for an hour or more. The object to the south was visible for two or three hours and beamed down a stream of light from time to time. Numerous individuals, including the undersigned, witnessed the activities in paragraphs 2 and 3.

CHARLES I. HALT, Lt Col, USAF
Deputy Base Commander

This formerly classified brief describes "Unexplained Lights" coming from Rendlesham Forest.

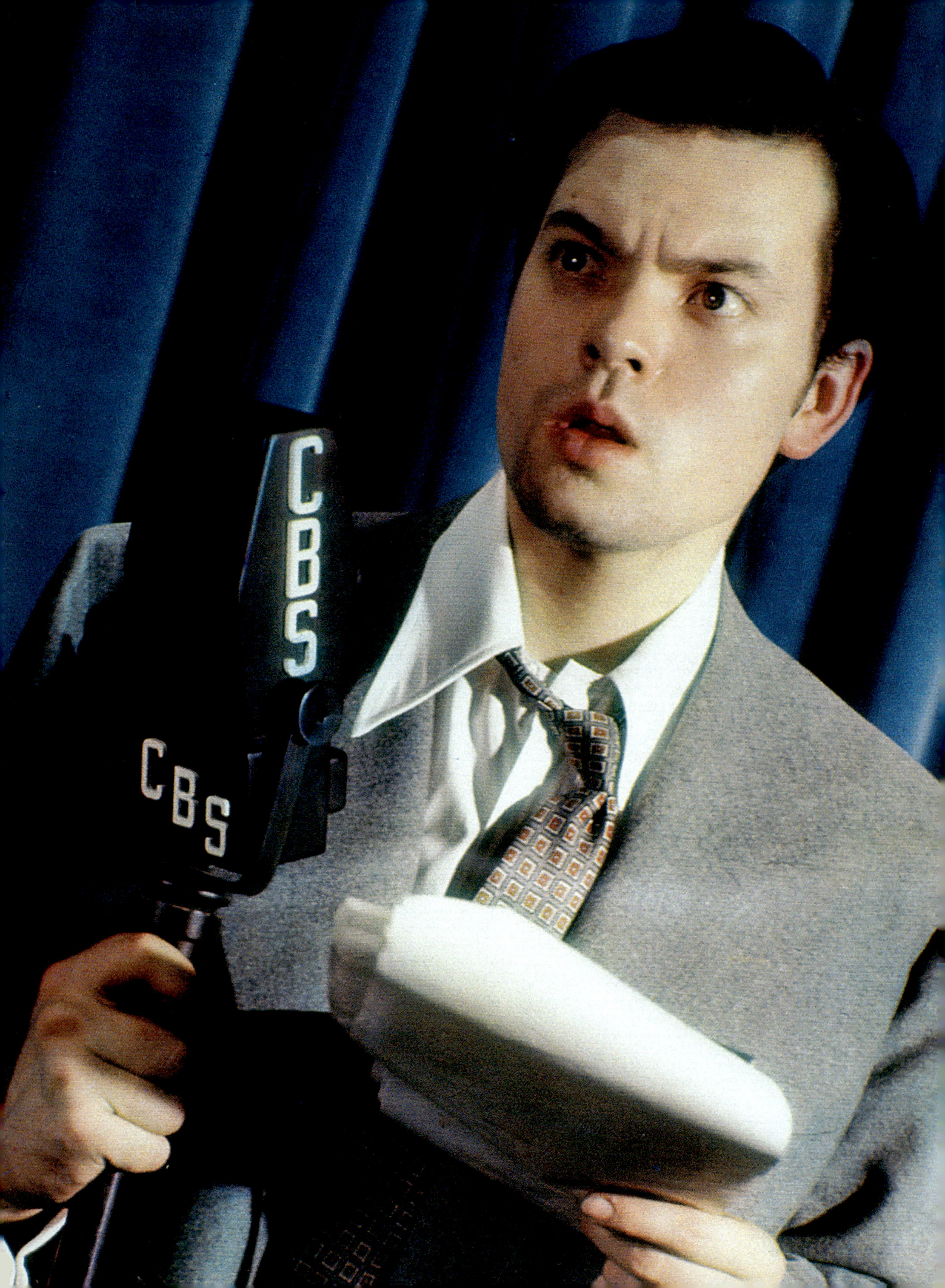
CBS
CBS

5

THE SKIES ARE FALLING!

"New York has been destroyed! It's the end of the world! Go home and prepare to die!"

ANONYMOUS WOMAN ON THE EVENING OF
ORSON WELLES'S *WAR OF THE WORLDS* RADIO BROADCAST

HUMAN HISTORY IS FULL OF EXAMPLES of strangers visiting unsuspecting Natives—from the Romans visiting the cultures outside the Mediterranean in the early centuries CE to Europeans arriving on the shore of the Americas in the fifteenth century. Unfortunately, when humans arrive in a new place, they tend to want to take what they find through any means. When strangers come, disease, looting, and war tend to follow.

Imagine, then, if all of humanity were the Natives, and an alien civilization arrived on Earth. It's possible they may be a peace-loving race of creatures, hoping to connect with another planet across the huge, cold, and empty expanse of space. However, if

Opposite: Orson Welles at the radio production of *The War of the Worlds*

they're anything like humans, that may be the opposite of their intentions. The day before Halloween, 1938, saw exactly the kind of mass hysteria that might follow an invasion of hostile aliens.

The Man Behind the Hysteria

The mastermind behind the spooky Halloween radio broadcast was the American actor, director, and writer Orson Welles. Welles was the producer of *The Mercury Theatre on the Air*, the radio version of his popular theatre company Mercury Theatre, which broadcast hour-long performances of works of literature. During its six months on the air, listeners heard performances of such classics as Shakespeare's *Julius Caesar*, Bram Stoker's *Dracula*, Sir Arthur Conan Doyle's *Sherlock Holmes*, and many more.

In preparation for Halloween, Welles got the idea to adapt the novel *The War of the Worlds* by H.G. Wells for his program. *The War of the Worlds* tells the story of the people of Earth after a civilization of hostile aliens lands and starts to kill people. Instead of simply reading from the book, Welles imagined performing it with a group of studio actors. Welles would play the role of a news reporter interrupting a regular broadcast to deliver a field report, and the other actors would perform as civilians, police officers, and soldiers witnessing the event.

The "Invasion"

The broadcast started like many other radio programs of the day. A reporter gave a weather report before turning things over to an orchestra to play dance music. However, a few moments after the orchestra had started to play, a newsman (played by Welles) interrupted the performance. The newsman's bulletin said that "Professor Farrell of the Mount Jenning Observatory" had reported seeing explosions on the surface of Mars. The program then turned back to the orchestra, only to be interrupted again with another bulletin about a meteor crashing in a field in Grover's Mill, which is a real town in New Jersey.

The program was then taken over by the announcer, who described the crash site. The meteor, he said, turned out to be some sort of glowing cylinder—a spacecraft. A door to the craft opened, and the witnesses looked on in horror. The announcer described what lay inside:

> Good heavens, something's wriggling out of the shadow like a gray snake. Now it's another one, and another. They look like tentacles to me. There, I can see the thing's body. It's large, large as a bear and it glistens like wet leather. But that face, it … Ladies and gentlemen, it's indescribable. I can hardly force myself to keep looking at it. The eyes are black and gleam like a serpent. The mouth is V-shaped with saliva dripping from its rimless lips that seem to quiver and pulsate. The monster or whatever it is can hardly move. It seems weighed down by … possibly gravity or something. The thing's raising up. The crowd falls back now. They've seen plenty. This is the most extraordinary experience. I can't find words …

The Martians climbed out of their spacecraft and turned their weapons toward the gathering crowd. The newscaster reported that all of the soldiers who had formed a circle around the impact site were instantly vaporized—the aliens had used "heat-rays" to roast each of the soldiers until they were nothing but a pile of dust.

Dozens of reporters ask Orson Welles (seated, center) about his radio drama the day after its broadcast.

Panic

Although Welles's broadcast was introduced as a performance of *The War of the Worlds*, which should have tipped off listeners that the whole broadcast was a matter of fiction, many of its listeners missed the warning. Similar to the way people watch television today, people listening to radio in the 1930s often "channel surfed" during commercial breaks as they looked for something to listen to. By the time most of the program's listeners tuned in, Welles and his troupe of actors were already well into the account of aliens in New Jersey.

The performance was so convincing that the town of Grover's Mill, New Jersey, where the "invasion" was claimed to be taking place, and several other cities on the East Coast were swept up in mass panic. It is estimated that one million people heard the broadcast and believed that it was a true news story documenting an alien invasion. Cars jammed the highways out of town as people tried to flee. Police were flooded with requests for gas masks to protect people from the poisonous gas that the first wave of aliens was using to kill humans. One woman ran into a church in Indianapolis, Indiana, and shouted that Earth was under attack, New York had already been destroyed, and that aliens were coming to kill everyone.

On Halloween, the day after the broadcast, the people of the United States woke up relieved that they had lasted through the night. Orson Welles had become a household name for terrorizing millions with his convincing performance.

The Man on Mars

Mars was the source of the frightening aliens in Orson Welles's infamous radio broadcast. Although scientists haven't been able to spot any explosions on the planet's surface like "Professor Farrell" did, observers have recently found a puzzling structure on the face of the planet. This structure is called 035A72, better known as "The Face on Mars." On July 25, 1976, *Viking I*, an observational spacecraft NASA had launched to study the planet Mars, transmitted a photograph that startled scientists and captured the world's imagination. The photo seems to depict a huge rock formation shaped like a human face, complete with eyes, a nose, and mouth. People who believe in aliens on Mars point to the shocking symmetry of the features. They argue that such a structure could not have randomly formed through geological process but must be the creation of an intelligent alien race.

Skeptics beg to disagree. The Face on Mars is only a trick of the eye, called pareidolia, that causes people to see a familiar pattern where there is none. This interpretation has been supported by later space missions to Mars. Decades after the Viking mission, the *Mars Global Surveyor* (1997–2006) and the *Mars Reconnaissance Orbiter* (2006–) have both taken images of the same region of Mars that features the so-called "face." Both of these spacecraft have improved technology that allowed them to take high-quality three-dimensional images of the formation. Scientists have practically all agreed that these images depict just a mountain—no alien monument.

The Man on Mars

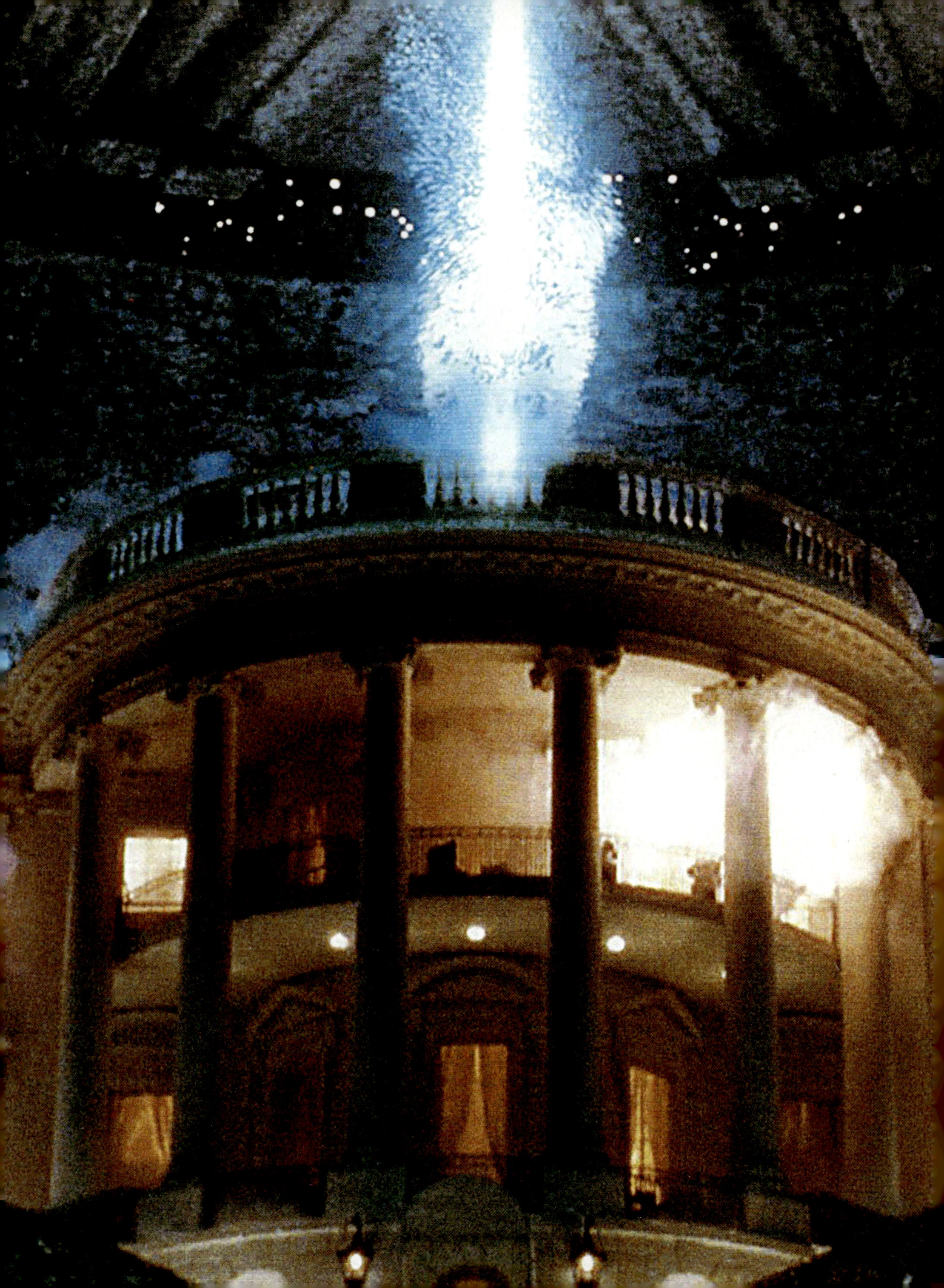

EXTRATERRESTRIALS IN FILM

"I saw what they're planning to do. They're like locusts. They're moving from planet to planet—their whole civilization. After they've consumed every natural resource, they move on ... and we're next. Nuke 'em."
BILL PULLMAN AS PRESIDENT THOMAS WHITMORE, *INDEPENDENCE DAY*

ALIENS HAVE BEEN POPULAR SUBJECTS FOR filmmakers since the beginning of cinema. During the 1950s, directors created movies that scared moviegoers with fantastic stories of alien invasions. Today, filmmakers such as J.J. Abrams and Stephen Spielberg continue the tradition. Using advanced computer-generated image technology, filmmakers can take our imaginations to even more incredible places, filled with lifelike beings that both terrify and delight audiences.

Hostile Extraterrestrials

As with the alien movies of the past, today aliens are a classic choice for horror movie directors. Limited only by their imagination,

Opposite: Scene from Independence Day

Actress Sigourney Weaver (*left*) **hides from the menacing creature in** *Alien*.

filmmakers can create some of the most terrifying creatures audiences have seen.

The 1979 movie *Alien* introduced movie fans to an especially horrifying creature. These aliens hatched from eggs and resembled huge crabs, which could jump onto a human face, smothering the victim and depositing an embryo into their body. The embryo would then explode from its host's chest cavity and quickly mature into a full-grown adult, an aggressive hunter that would stop at nothing to catch human prey. Indeed, it seemed built to hunt. It walked on two legs, making it fast and agile.

Its body was covered in a hard exoskeleton, it had sharp fangs, and its whip-like tail came to a point like a dagger. Even its blood was poisonous and corrosive.

Other times, aliens are threatening, not just for their frightening appearance but also for their technology, which is almost too sophisticated for human beings to defend against. This was the case in Roland Emmerich's *Independence Day* (1996) where the extraterrestrials wielded technology that wiped out large parts of the planet. The aliens from *Independence Day* traveled in huge spaceships that were the size of several city blocks. During their invasion, these ships positioned themselves over the world's major cities—Washington, DC, New York City, London, Paris, Moscow. In a coordinated assault, each ship opened doors at its bottom and released a beam of energy so powerful that it annihilated everything in its path.

Revealing the Human Spirit

Movies about horrifying aliens are often written not just to scare audiences but to show what our species is capable of in the face of hardship. If aliens have vastly superior weapons and enough ships to darken the skies over entire cities, what about us makes it possible to resist them? In many movies, such as *Independence Day*, it is the classic grit, determination, and resourcefulness that has allowed humans to survive for hundreds of thousands of years in a hostile world.

At the end of *Independence Day*, humanity seems to be on the ropes. The world's major cities have been destroyed, there are countless casualties, and the world's governments are forced into underground bunkers. Even the most powerful human weapons cannot scratch the alien spacecraft, because a mother ship orbiting Earth is protecting them all with a shield. All seems lost until scientist David Levinson, played by Jeff Goldblum, comes up with a daring solution: Levinson, along with Marine Corps pilot Captain Steven Hiller (played by Will Smith), will fly a captured alien spaceship into the mother ship and install a computer virus that will weaken the alien defenses, then explode the ship from the inside. It seems to be the world's best shot at salvation, but not everyone is sure. To encourage the remaining humans, United States President Thomas Whitmore, played by Bill Pullman, gives the following famous speech:

> In less than an hour, aircraft from here will join others from around the world, and you will be launching the largest aerial battle in the history of mankind … Mankind—that word should have new meaning for all of us today. We can't be consumed by our petty differences anymore. We will be united in our common interests. Perhaps it's fate that today is the

Fourth of July, and you will once again be fighting for our freedom—not from tyranny, oppression, or persecution—but from annihilation. We're fighting for our right to live, to exist. And should we win the day, the Fourth of July will no longer be known as an American holiday, but as the day when the world declared in one voice, "We will not go quietly into the night! We will not vanish without a fight! We're going to live on! We're going to survive!'" Today, we celebrate our Independence Day!

Whitmore's speech is one of the most famous movie speeches of all time, partly because it could apply to any number of other situations beyond an alien invasion. Much like the American independence movement in the eighteenth century, Pullman's *Independence Day* speech demonstrates that humans can rise to the occasion no matter the odds.

Friendly Aliens

E.T.'s glowing heart proves that not all aliens are scary.

Filmmakers do not always portray aliens as terrifying monsters out for global annihilation. Two of the most famous movies that feature alien life-forms are Stephen Spielberg's *Close Encounters of the Third Kind* (1977) and *E.T. the Extra-Terrestrial* (1982). The appearance of the extraterrestrials in *Close Encounters* was modeled after real-life accounts of alien abductions and has become accepted as common in popular culture. The creatures have small bodies, smooth gray skin, large hairless heads on long, thin necks, and slanted eyes. While they have abducted Earthlings in the past, it seems to be out of curiosity rather than malice. And these alien beings attempt to communicate with the people they meet through a musical sequence and a series of hand gestures—they even imitate a smile when they see one. Compared to the monster from *Alien*, E.T. is a cuddly teddy bear. He has a pudgy body with a heart that glows warmly, and his only desire is to go back to his home planet.

Aliens and the Past

Like most types of monsters, the fear that aliens can instill is often used as a mirror to point out what it is about ourselves that should scare us. Whatever it is that an alien in a movie is shown to do—be it murdering a human, performing diabolical medical experiments, or capturing human civilization and bending it to its will—these are all things that we ourselves are capable of.

A good example of this is the 2009 movie *Avatar*, which was directed by James Cameron. *Avatar* seems to turn the theme of marauding aliens visiting Earth to destroy Earthlings and use up the planet's resources on its head. In *Avatar*, it is humans who come to visit the alien world of Pandora, where they find a vein of fictional precious metal called unobtainium. In their quest to mine it, they come in direct conflict with the local Na'vi, who must fight to protect their home from the alien humans.

This story of discovery and ruthless exploitation is a common one in human history. Look no further than the treatment of the Native people of Central and South America during the Age of Discovery in the fifteenth and sixteenth centuries. Much like the Na'vi, Native cultures such as the Aztecs in Mexico and the Incas in Peru thrived in a secluded world that was blessed with abundant natural resources. When the Spanish arrived and discovered gold there, they waged all-out war, wiping out much of these cultures in their thirst for riches. While aliens may be used to frighten us, it is also possible that these stories are meant to teach us as well.

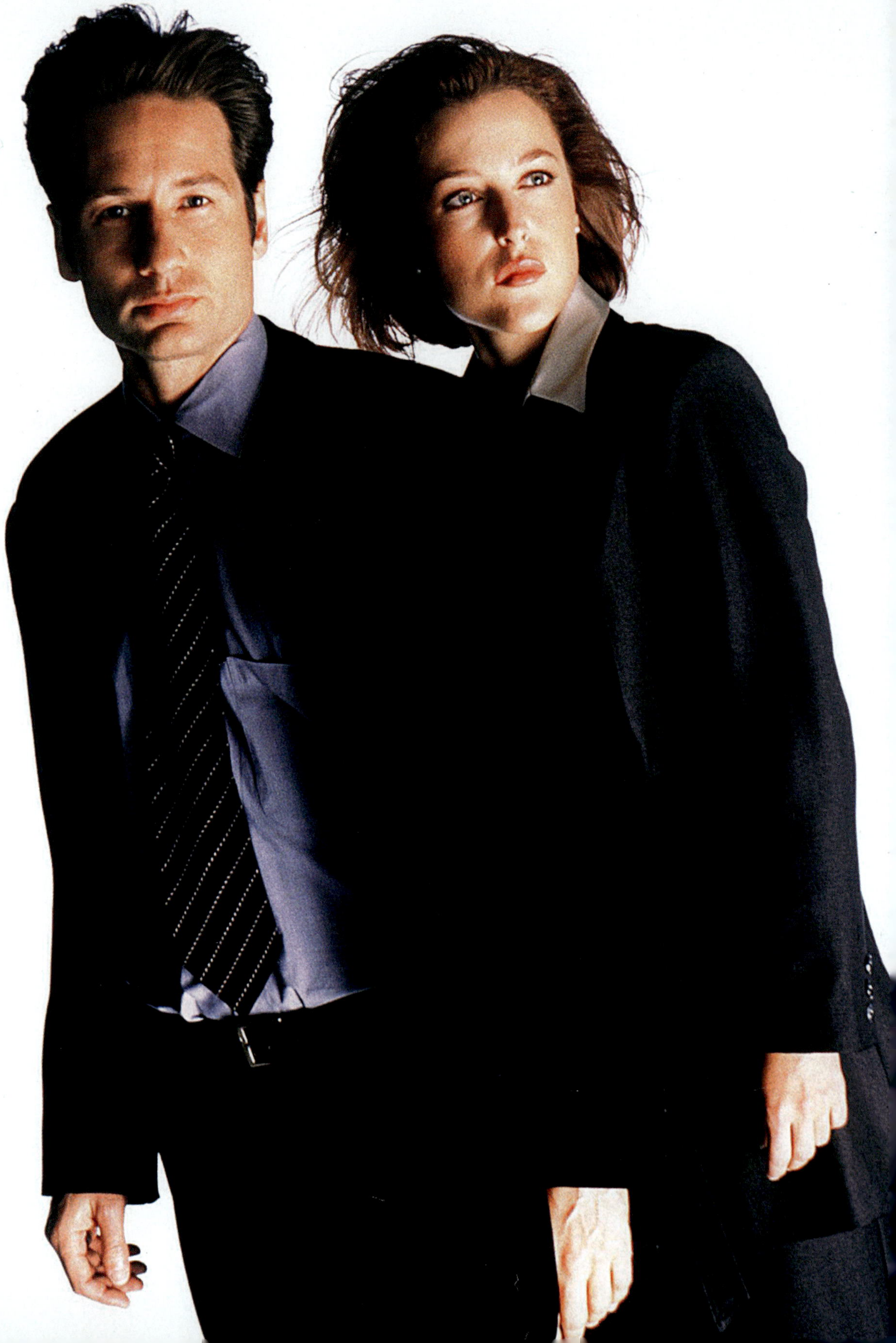

7

ALIENS AMONG US

"The truth is out there."
THE X-FILES

ALTHOUGH ALIENS HAVE BEEN A MAJOR PART of American pop culture for decades, they are not without controversy. On the one hand, extraterrestrials are responsible for billions of dollars' worth of spending. Americans willingly consume books, television shows, movies, and other media related to aliens, buy alien merchandise, and visit places that aliens have allegedly visited. However, while aliens are a major part of culture, those who actually believe in them are often stigmatized, or made to feel disgraced.

Alien Pop Culture

If the way people spend money points to how they feel, Americans would seem to love aliens. Few other fantastic creatures seem

Opposite: David Duchovny and Gillian Anderson play FBI agents in *The X-Files.*

to draw as much attention and money as aliens, and many of the most successful movies and TV shows feature aliens. One of the most successful alien-inspired shows in the 1990s and early 2000s was *The X-Files*. It followed two FBI agents on their fight to unearth the truth about alien life. A box-office movie based on the show debuted in 1998. It had tremendous success, making $30 million in its opening weekend. In 2015, *The X-Files* was reprised as a TV show, featuring many of the original cast members, after a thirteen-year break.

James Cameron's movie *Avatar* has made almost $2.8 billion since its release in 2009, making it the highest-grossing movie to date. Aliens also figure prominently in the most successful media franchises. A recent ranking of the history's top movie franchises by the business magazine *Forbes* put four alien-related film series within the top fifteen: *Star Trek* at thirteenth, *Transformers* at tenth, *Star Wars* at third, and the Marvel Cinematic Universe at number one. Combined, these franchises pulled in nearly $7.5 billion.

Many of these movie franchises, such as *Star Wars* and *Star Trek*, also have a huge cult following. For these fans, it is not enough to enjoy the alien universe depicted in these shows; they want to live them. Perhaps the most famous group of fans are the so-called "Trekkies," the common term for *Star Trek*'s fan following. Trekkies often dress up to attend conventions to meet like-minded enthusiasts. One hardcore subset of Trekkies are those who dress, speak, and act like Klingons, an alien race that figures prominently in the *Star Trek* universe. In fact, the Klingon language is so developed throughout the *Star Trek* franchise that many serious fans have studied it well enough to actually speak it themselves as if it were a modern human language.

The Dark Side of Alien Belief

While the majority of Americans are more than happy to support the idea of aliens as long as they are limited to fictionalized settings like movies, those who actually believe that alien life forms exist and have visited Earth are often the target of ridicule by the wider population. At best, those who openly admit to believing in aliens may be ignored; however, in some cases, alien belief is made out to be a form of mental illness. Those who believe they have had a **close encounter** with extraterrestrial life are often made to feel like outsiders—alien even among their own kind.

Although psychologists have been unable to determine whether all of those who claim they have been abducted by aliens suffer from mental illness, that doesn't keep the majority from suggesting abductees are out of their minds. Abductees are often diagnosed with mental disorders such as bipolar disorder, delusion disorder, paranoia, schizophrenia, and narcissistic personality disorder, where an individual thinks that they have been the subject of alien tests because they are special. Because many abductees often aren't diagnosed with a mental disorder prior to their experience, it is difficult to determine whether their stories are merely symptoms of an illness or if their experiences actually happened.

Conspiracy Theories

Because alien belief is so closely associated with paranoia, many who believe in aliens are also considered to be conspiracy theorists. To them, extraterrestrials are real, and the reason aliens' existence is not more widely accepted is because they are the target of a coordinated effort by certain organizations to keep the truth from getting out. Some tame theories hold that government agencies such as the CIA

Actors in *Signs* wear tin foil hats.

actively conceal and destroy evidence of alien activity. Others are more extreme, alleging that shadowy organizations are behind the cover-ups, or that extraterrestrials themselves manipulate people's memories and perceptions through brain control.

Some of the more extreme conspiracy theorists can be identified by their peculiar headgear: tinfoil hats. These helmets are said to prevent aliens from reading and manipulating the wearer's mind by blocking electromagnetic radiation. The tinfoil hat makes an appearance in the movie *Signs* (2002). Tinfoil hats were once so prevalent that the term became shorthand for anything relating to conspiracy theories or delusions.

The Mothman of West Virginia

In November 1966, the town of Point Pleasant, West Virginia, was rocked by sightings of a mysterious creature. On Wednesday, November 16, two couples called the police, saying that they had seen a creature near an abandoned power plant outside of town. They described the creature as being between 6 and 7 feet (1.8 and 2 m) tall. It was gray in color and had a wingspan of 10 feet (3 m). Perhaps its most distinguishing feature was its huge, red eyes that glowed when light hit them. The couples were startled by the creature, but when they turned to drive away, it leapt into the air and hovered over their car. The *Point Pleasant Register* reported the story in an article titled, "Couples See Man-Sized Bird … Creature … Something."

Over the next few days, many more Point Pleasant citizens, including two firefighters and the sheriff, reported seeing what became known as Mothman. Several of these sightings were connected to UFOs, suggesting that Mothman may have been an alien being lurking in the woods.

Later that month, Dr. Robert L. Smith, associate professor of wildlife biology at West Virginia University, proposed that Mothman was merely a sandhill crane that had wandered from its migration route. Sandhill cranes are native to the United States, can grow to about 5 feet (1.5 m), have a wingspan of 7 feet (2 m), and feature bright red skin around each eye. This would seem to account for all of the descriptions that had been reported about Mothman. Nevertheless, alleged sightings of Mothman continue even today in the dark back roads of Point Pleasant, West Virginia.

Glossary

abduct To take someone, as by aliens, against their will.

classified A word describing objects, such as documents or evidence, that has been officially designated as secret, viewable only by specially authorized persons.

close encounter An encounter with extraterrestrial life or an unidentified flying object.

conspiracy A secret plan by a group to do something illegal. In regards to aliens, a conspiracy is an attempt made by the government to conceal information about extraterrestrial life.

conspiracy theorist Someone who believes that a secret group is behind certain events, such as the Roswell, New Mexico, incident.

cover-up An alternate but false story given to conceal the true nature of an event.

crop circle A pattern made in a field of standing crops by flattening the stalks in a circle, pattern, or other design. Many people believe that crop circles are formed by extraterrestrials, but many have been confirmed to be man-made.

debunk To prove false.

deep space The space outside of Earth's atmosphere.

extraterrestrial A being from outside Earth's atmosphere.

galaxy A gravitational system containing billions of stars and planets along with dust and gas.

hoax A lie.

light-year The distance light can travel in one year, which is approximately 5.88 trillion miles (9.46 trillion km).

mass The quantity of matter that makes up an organism.

organism A life form, be it an animal, plant, or single-celled being.

phenomenon An unexplained occurrence that is observed by people.

skeptic A person who doubts the claims of another.

solar system The name of a group of planets, moons, asteroids, and other material that orbits around a sun.

UFO An acronym that stands for "unidentified flying object," one of a number of bodies observed in the sky that cannot be determined.

To Learn More About Aliens

Books

Alexander, John B. *UFOs: Myths, Conspiracies, and Realities.* New York: Thomas Dunne Books, 2011.

Hynek, J. Allen. *The UFO Experience: A Scientific Inquiry.* New York: Marlowe & Company, 1972.

Kean, Leslie. *UFOs: Generals, Pilots, and Government Officials Go on the Record.* New York: Harmony Books, 2010.

Website

Ancient Aliens on the History Channel
www.history.com/shows/ancient-aliens

Discover the official website for the History Channel's popular show *Ancient Aliens*, which considers the ancient astronaut theory.

Circlemakers
www.circlemakers.org

This is the official website of the Circlemakers, an England-based organization that is "making the world a more interesting place." Here, you can read articles, view photos, and watch videos about their work.

Videos

Avatar. Directed by James Cameron. 20th Century Fox, 2009. DVD.

E.T. the Extraterrestrial. Directed by Stephen Spielberg. Universal Pictures, 1982. DVD.

Bibliography

"1947 Roswell UFO Incident." RoswellUFOMuseum.com. Accessed November 9, 2015. http://www.roswellufomuseum.com/incident.html.

Boyle, Alan. "Area 51 and its purpose declassified: No UFOs, but lots of U-2 spy planes. NBCnews.com. Accessed November 9, 2015. http://www.nbcnews.com/science/area-51-its-purpose-declassified-no-ufos-lots-u-2-6C10931555.

Coppens, Philip. *The Ancient Alien Question: A New Inquiry Into the Existence, Evidence, and Influence of Ancient Visitors.* Pompton Plains, NJ: The Career Press, 2012.

Friedman, Stanton T. *Captured! The Betty and Barney Hill UFO Experience: The True Story of the World's First Documented Alien Abduction.* Franklin Lakes, NJ: The Career Press, 2007.

Hynek, J. Allen. *The UFO Experience: A Scientific Inquiry.* New York: Marlowe & Company, 1972.

Jacobsen, Annie. *Area 51: An Uncensored History of America's Top Secret Military Base.* New York: Little, Brown and Company, 2011.

Kean, Leslie. *UFOs: Generals, Pilots, and Government Officials Go on the Record.* New York: Harmony Books, 2010.

McCarthy, Niall. "The Most Successful Movie Franchises in History." Forbes.com. Accessed November 9, 2015. http://www.forbes.com/sites/niallmccarthy/2015/04/13/the-most-successful-movie-franchises-in-history-infographic.

Pope, Nick. *Encounter in Rendlesham Forest: The Inside Story of the World's Best-Documented UFO Incident.* New York: Thomas Dunne Books, 2014.

Swanson, Emily. "Alien Poll Finds Half of Americans Think Extraterrestrial Life Exists." HuffingtonPost.com. Accessed November 9, 2015. http://www.huffingtonpost.com/2013/06/21/alien-poll_n_3473852.html.

Turner, Ralph. "That Mothman: Would You Believe a Sandhill Crane?" WVculture.org. Accessed November 9, 2015. http://www.wvculture.org/history/notewv/mothman3.jpg.

von Däniken, Erich. Trans. Michael Heron. *Chariots of the Gods: Unsolved Mysteries of the Past.* New York: Berkley Books, 1999.

Index

Page numbers in **boldface** are illustrations. Entries in **boldface** are glossary terms.

abduct, 25–28, **27**, 50, 57

classified, 29, 41
close encounter, 57
conspiracy, 36, 57–58
conspiracy theorist, 36, 57–58
cover-up, 36, 38, 40, 58
crop circle, 31, **31**

debunk, 29, 36
deep space, 12

extraterrestrial, 10–12, 14, 19, 22–23, 25, 28, 30–31, 36, 49–50, 52, 55, 57–58

Face on Mars, 47, **47**

galaxy, 10–11, **11**, 13–14

Hawking, Stephen, 10
Hill, Barney and Betty, 26–27, 40
hoax, 27, 30–31

light-year, 10–11

Mars, 22, **22**, 45, 47,
Martians, 22, 45
mass, 12

movie aliens, 21–22, 49–53, **50**, 52, **52**, 53, 56, 58

Nazca lines, 20–21, **21**

organism, 12, 15
origin myths, 17–18
   ancient astronaut theory, 19–20

phenomenon, 30
Project Mogul, 37

radio waves, 11–12, 15
Rendlesham Forest, **32**, 33, 37–41
Roswell, NM, 33–38, 40

skeptic, 27, 47
solar system, 9–13, 15, 22
space shuttle, 12–13, **13**
spacecraft, 12, 23, **24**, 29, 35–37, 39–40, 45, 47, 51
Star Trek, 56
Stonehenge, 19, **19**

UFO, 26, 28–30, 33, 35, 37, 40, 59

War of the Worlds, 22, 43–46, 50
Welles, Orson, **42**, 44, 46–47, **46**

X-Files, The, **54**, 56

About the Author

Andrew Coddington holds a degree in creative writing from Canisius College. He formerly worked in publishing as an editor. He has written several books, including *Ghosts* and *Demons* in the Creatures of Fantasy series. Coddington lives in Lancaster, New York, where the clear skies give him the perfect chance to spot lights in the night.

Indian Trail Jr. High LRC
Addison, IL